SILENCE FELL

silence fell

JOSEPHINE DICKINSON

HOUGHTON MIFFLIN COMPANY   BOSTON   NEW YORK

2007

Visit our Web site: www.houghtonmifflinbooks.com.

Library of Congress Cataloging-in-Publication Data
Dickinson, Josephine.
Silence fell / Josephine Dickinson.
p. cm.
ISBN-13: 978-0-618-71871-9
ISBN-10: 0-618-71871-0
1. Farm life — Poetry. I. Title.
PR6104.I25S56 2007
821'.92 — dc22   2006026868

Book design by Melissa Lotfy

Printed in the United States of America

MP 10 9 8 7 6 5 4 3 2 1

For Douglas

•

DOUGLAS DICKINSON

HILL FARMER

OCTOBER 5, 1911—MARCH 15, 2004

My Heart ran so to thee

EMILY DICKINSON

CONTENTS

FOREWORD

I first met Josephine Dickinson at a reading in 2004 at the Morden Tower, Northumberland. My wife, Bobbie Bristol, who had been seated beside Josephine at a dinner the day before, introduced us and we spoke briefly. On the plane back to the United States Bobbie and I read her books, *Scarberry Hill* and *The Voice*, both published in England. We liked them very much. *Silence Fell* carries forward the narrative thread of those two books. Set on Alston Moor, a wild remote landscape in the Cumbrian high Pennines, it tells the story of an unusual marriage, and also, in the words of the author, "the story of my coming to Scarberry Hill, making my life here, my engagement with the secrets of this small world, secrets as real as those of the South Pole."

I mailed the books to Houghton Mifflin, my publisher. They were eager to publish a selection from both books but felt that for an American audience something needed to be said about the locale and the person who wrote the poems. So when I was on a reading tour in Scotland half a year later, I took an excursion to Alston.

I drove across the Eden Valley, passing signs for hamlets and villages such as Little Salkeld, Unthank, and Gamblesby, and woods and corners with names such as Whinny Brow, Nettle Hole, and Sweet Wells. After the village of Melmerby, a steep climb of nearly two thousand feet up the sheer side of a mountain begins. A sign warns drivers to take care as they negotiate the innumerable switchbacks. Here and there on the green moraines are straggles of black-faced sheep. There are no barriers except a few chicken-wire fences and broken stone walls. On the western horizon the silhouette of the Lake District mountains stands clear. The landscape and its singular names evoke for me something of the spirit of Josephine's poems.

I saw the remains of a Roman way that chutes straight up the mountainside. From the top of the pass I could see the distant shimmer of Solway Firth, and beyond it Scotland. From then on, the road is less kinked and descends for several miles at a gentle gradient. As the road emerges between Black Fell and Fiend's Fell, the town of Alston appears in its valley. Here a population of about two thousand has been shaped by long centuries of isolation and hardship and by the cultures of sheep farming and lead mining. Recently there has been an influx of artists and writers.

Josephine lives two miles out of Alston, on the other side of the valley. Here I found her with two cats and a Border collie. Her cottage was named Scarberry Hill by her late husband, Douglas, and when I looked out a window I could see why: it has a tremendous wide view over the river valley toward Scarberry Hill in the west.

Josephine was about to feed her sheep when I arrived. In the barn she emptied the contents of a fifty-pound sack of sheep rolls and a sack of pellets into a bin and scooped out a bucketful. On to the Flatt Field we went, where her twenty-eight sheep were waiting. There was total silence as every one of them looked at her with rapt attention. She took the bucket to the end of a feeder. I wondered how she was going to feed the sheep, which looked to be almost the size of buffalo, without getting squashed. Moving quickly, she poured the feed from the bucket and started running, pouring the feed as she ran.

Afterward, I went along on the walk she takes every day. A lane took us down to the South Tyne River. We crossed a shepherd's bridge and passed a ford where many years ago, Josephine said, Douglas would drive his cattle. The river takes on the hue of whichever of the great slabs of rock it slides over. The first coltsfoot flowers of spring were beginning to appear on the banks. Scotch pine, wych elm, alder, ash, and willow trees leaned over the water. We climbed up steep wooden steps set into the side of the ravine on the other side. We clambered over two tall stone walls using their ingenious built-in stiles. We passed an ancient fallen stone house called Silly Hall, which someone was in the process of restoring.

Josephine, who became profoundly deaf overnight at the age of six, tried to give me an idea of how she experiences language and words: "It's as if, when I see and write words, I experience their sound, rhythm, and meaning with my whole body, not just with my mouth or ears. And when lip-reading, I am looking at the whole person, not just the lips." I found that the more she and I talked, the more easily she understood my words, until soon I forgot entirely that she was deaf. She would say "I beg your pardon?" no more frequently than I, slightly deaf myself, would say, "Could you say that again?"

I asked about the connection between becoming deaf and turning to poetry. "Well," she said, "I started to experience life in a different way. It's true that, having been a gregarious, ebullient child, I became isolated in some ways and the written word became increasingly vital, but what is more important is that I was able to discover that the possible range of human experience is so vast that in losing one sense, one gains a new dimension in the others. From where I now was, I saw language and words as just another aspect of being alive, something to be hungry for, yes, but also an actual concrete element, a medium to be used. I had no choice but to experience my life in an intensified way, and it was natural for me that it should be poems that brought me to this realization."

Josephine grew up in South London, read classics at Oxford, and studied music. After a spell as a composer and a community arts worker, during which time she continued to write poems and began to publish them, she moved to Alston in 1994. Here, in 1998, while searching for some lost geese, she came upon a retired, widowed farmer, Douglas Dickinson, in his late eighties (she was forty-one at the time), living alone at Scarberry Hill. It was March, and lambing was already under way. They married and lived six years together, until his death in March 2004. Many of the poems were written for an audience of one, for Douglas, who loved poetry and whose own speech was rich with the local Cumberland intonation and vocabulary, and full of music and quirky wit. In her words, Douglas "took me into his life of sheep and the harshness of rocks and weather and the beauty of trees and rivers and healed much that was wrong with me at the time." In turn, Josephine tried to be a traditional northern wife, cared for Douglas as he faded away, and all the while wrote these poems.

When I read Josephine's poems on the plane back from Britain, I saw in them the same vitality and humor I had found in her. In my many subsequent readings, I discovered feats of technique and intellect, and emotional depths, and a passionate attachment to the things of the world that I had not seen immediately.

To begin with, she has a fondness for one- and two-syllable Anglo-Saxon and early English words, some exclusive to the region, and her startlingly precise use of them can make a poem jump off the page. She is speaking here of gathering mushrooms:

> We glean the four that glow, gray-gilled,
> leave black side up in the muck the maggoty ones,

Sometimes her syntax seems to stop time by withholding the meaning of a sentence until its very last word:

> He gave me the note
> the blackbird
> I'd cried at the blackness of
> by the river sang.

Applying a rich sense of humor and a reckless artfulness, she deals aslant with a topic that might well pop into a reader's head:

> the weight will throw you flat as a "Li*ve* '*ere? Grrra*nd!"
> in a de*via-gra*m,
> albeit in gorgeous surroundings (*vie aggra*vatingly for
> them!). [italics added]

She also has the power to speak quietly and fully and lovingly, as in
this passage of empathy between species, a human and a donkey:

> I sat under her chin
> and let her chew my hair.
> I ran my fingers up and down
> her forelegs till clumps of down
> drifted away. She paused,
> then continued to pull
> and surround with her mouth
> the tufts of grass.

The power of human love is never far away. It permeates all of the
poems, as in these lines from "Breathing":

> As I sit in another room you are swishing your lips.
> You have become the inside of my body.

Sometimes a bitter note appears:

> The sun changes.
> Your eyes are blue.
> You are cruel.
> But your words are true.

Sometimes we feel the pleasurable shock of a piercing image:

> Cow with a sad bull yells like a chainsaw.

She has a sharp ear for the raw suggestiveness of language — as here,
where she conveys almost the whole meaning by sounds alone:

> Freaks!
>   Jag, tug, wrench.
> With nippers, winkle out,
>   mumble, champ and peck.
> It'll do. Just tucker.

This ewe lamb
        is in the clouds,
    giddy with thinking
            of wool in the spring.
A wobbler, a blink, a dimp.

If asked whether Josephine Dickinson's poems are accessible — horrible word when applied to poetry — I might after my first reading have said, "Yes, completely." Now I would say that they beckon — that faithful Old English word. The reader can enter them, delight in them, and sometimes not be able to find a way out, as if a word were missing where there could be no word, or a transformation had happened that cannot be explained.

GALWAY KINNELL
Sheffield, Vermont
July 2006

SILENCE FELL

Down Two Fields

Down two fields
to where, between
two woods, a little

house stood, smoke
rising silently,
I waded through

the grass and weeds,
vaulted over a swing
gate, there I was.

Through the gate,
down the path,
knock the door,

you open it,
eyes wide,
nod me in.

You perch in your high
throne like a sparrow, talk
in your chirrupy squeak.

I have no idea why
I find it so moving.
That's just life.

We sit in silence,
legs crossed, one
each side of the fire.

You have your pipe
squeezed into your
mouth, eyes

clouded, far away,
looking down like
the crow for scraps

now and again,
scraps of looks, affection.
You are loving me.

Sometimes you think
about the sheep. Sometimes
just sit and think.

The sharp suck of smoke,
the nip of lips,
is the only sound.

The sudden outpoured light
on Scarberry Hill
the only drama.

I think of your face, and how
I would draw the eyes.
Like that great

poet of Russia, Akhmatova,
they look down, proud,
vulnerable.

We sit a long time in silence,
my head resting on your shoulder.
Smoke meanders from your smouldering
pipe, high into the air over
my head. I look sideways at Scar-
berry Hill, the dark bands rippling
slowly down its side, at the wind-
sock in the garden rising and
falling in a halfhearted sigh.
The door is locked, the fire built and
glowing. No one else near. We sit
and watch the changing sky moving.

March

I heard the owl hoot this morning,
from the haunted farm come down
to the wood.
— D. D.

Wherever you fly, whatever you do,
perched on the sheep pen, hid in the reeds
near the sheep with your mate, or soaring as two,
eyes down for your food,

though he made up his mind to leave that day,
the thirteenth of March — what's more, Friday —
and we kissed goodbye as if for all eternity
— which it came to be —

and I was alone in the haunted house
and slammed the door as I left to go
down the field through the dark March cold of night,
and you visited — twice,

and the geese led me on a hinny goose chase,
for I'd let them out — big mistake —
seen wonderful sight of wings in flight,
mysterious, white,

and you visit me now, swoop over my head,
seven times circling, wings outspread,
and we scrutinize each the other's face
through your ruffled hood,

I'm at the top of the world here, brought by you
with your feathered claws gripped tight at my breast,
your knowing eyes turned round to look
at mine and the rest of the world,

and around us the fells on all four sides —
Cross Fell, Middle Fell, Clarghyll Head, Gilderdale,
and the Horse Pasture at the edge of the world —
all face, never meet.

Apple Pie

He wanted her. So did she spend the rest
of her life making apple pie? The wood
lured her. She wandered under a high hedge,
so high the light was scarcely able to
penetrate. What was it made her draw near?
At what moment did her desire to know
outweigh her fear? The wizard lived behind
the high hedge. He lived alone. He got her.
She was lost in the wood. Why? Because it
was a fine day and the ground underfoot
was dry and satisfying to tread on.
Because one thing after another drew
her on. She knew an old wizard lived there.
Because she was simply lost in the wood,
drawn by the high hedge and its mystery
to see what was in it from a distance
then close up. At what point did his eyes look
out and meet hers looking in? Had he watched
for her or did she stumble on his guard?
How did he get her? Did she want to go?
What happened then? What were her thoughts? Did she
change with the seasons and did she love him?
We know he made her make him apple pie.
How did they live? Did he have an orchard?
Question: was the reality between
the reality outside the hedge and

the world of the potential behind it
fiction, or were the trees outside the high
hedge a dream whilst against the trees he seemed
very small but inside the world was real?

Scarberry Hill

Inside the house is silence. We sit and look
across the room. You shift your elbows, smoke
and tap your pipe by turns. I write my words
in my little book. We look across the room,
or read, or meet to talk from time to time.
On Scarberry Hill the shadow under the white cloud spreads
and rolls our way. It's far away. Perhaps
it won't come down this far before it stops —
above the whitewashed house, the tumbling river
washing the valley below. Perhaps we have
to wait until it passes over. Just
a bit of rain, that's all. And when it's past,
the sun will shine again. The windsock pulls
to east. It might yet rain. The moment stays.
As tiny cars are shuttling, changing place
across its darkening pastures, Scarberry Hill
appears to frown. You're shuffling papers round,
I'm writing in my notebook still. It passes.
On Scarberry Hill the blinding streaks of green
flood out, the sky's all sun, we wipe our glasses.

April

"It's fucking April." Light showers (old flames), seeded
by footsteps, laughter, light. Three lambs born in the night
(cold and bright). We feed the sheep. Count lambs. Quiet lunch. Go
out to see lambs, feed colostrum. Plant potatoes.
Sow seeds: chamomile, valerian, rosemary,
thyme, sea holly, hyssop. Up early. Douglas goes
to see lambs. Comes back. Two lambs dead. "Lambs will have died
all over the country." Surviving lamb not good.
In stable. Is being fed milk. Later we feed
it, but "it will be no good." We pick daffodils,
flowering currant, shift tulips, plant gladioli,
talk about seeds. In the greenhouse I dig, Douglas
rakes. Put cucumber seeds in pots, then lettuce, spring
cabbage, beetroot, brussels. Walk round, look for seedlings.
Too bad a day for gardening. Pet lamb arrives.
Douglas holds a hand up to warn me. It's poking
its black nose round the kitchen. Parked on bum in bin
on newspaper for night. Crying. Stops when I run
the tap. Next day take him to ewe. She's wild. But
lamb sucks, seems OK. Next day not sucking plenty.
Next day the ewe breaks out of the lamb adopter.
Next day the lamb is dead. We bury it. "We are
two children trying to prove there is life after
death." We feed the lambs in Billy's Field. Clip sheep's tails.
Quite a job. Next day we move all the sheep into
Billy's Field, mend gate, put flagstones down. Whistle sheep,
run down field, shout "Hope! Hope! Hope!" Slowly they follow.

The Bargain

D: I won't treat you as a deaf person.
J: Well, I won't treat you as being eighty-seven.

If saying I am deaf can make it so,
and we must not admit you're eighty-seven,
and you think not I might not hear you go
today when, cold and tired, you leave the garden
suddenly (we're staking wire against
the rabbits with Jackson, you say "Three's a crowd"
and slip away, enticed by pipe and stove,
I stay and splice the jagged nets, in the end,
with bleeding fingertips, alone), and love
does not convince us, either, we have good
intentions: deafness then can be my one
defense, your age becomes a toothless weapon.
Deaf, I hear, approve, forgive your laugh,
and you in turn have cut your age in half.

Do I Sleep with You?

Do I sleep with you or you with me?
It's splitting hairs to say I came to you
and use your brush and comb, and therefore we
don't "sleep together." But it may be true.
In any case, I say you sleep with me.
The action's mostly yours. You made me stay.
Made staying perfect, future and to be.
Apart from that, it's what most people say.
Tributaries join rivers, but they mix,
go to somewhere, neither cares to where.
Both stand and swell their bank beside a tree.
They're not concerned with any verbal tricks.
So, say I joined your river, if you dare.
In any case, I say you sleep with me.

The Red and the Blue

You wonder, am I satisfied with you?
Some inequality you take as read.
But raveling my hemp, your wool, my red,
your blue, we spin a single human hair.

May

"This is as good as it's going to get," you say. I disagree.
Chance is a leap towards serendipity.
Proud as a peacock, mushrooming with Cage,
once done, forgotten. One thing to do: declaim
Isaac Newton on the train. Take
a box and measure it. The place is a wreck,
and when you pick, wild-eyed, the pieces up
and shake them and see, you lose some, gain some, tossed
in the air, from the bits that landed here somewhere,
and try to make something good and true and new.
It's May: we sweep stray hayseeds up and pack
them in a sack and scatter them over peaty gleys
and podzols. Something different: plant twelve willows.
Bleagate bedroom: watch the nesting swallows.
Talk about being right on! You're a right-on teddy —
sorry, tiger — you're politically correct. Butter up my nibbles
and I'll give you a Helmut Schmidt (a helpful flit).
She sucks those sweet flowers to make her voice clear. The more
she sings cuckoo the summer draws near (the red and the blue).
Even in a bombed-out city there's a chance to build
again. I do not take my medicine.
I have a good cry. The grass looks extra green.
Rains like heaven. Shocked by religion. Ice cream
at seven. Coffee at eight. Then wine. Then bed,
very tired, and sleep all night and finally wake.
Lie a long time, still. "I slept all through the night,"
I say. You say, "You are better." Very happy. Why?

He Wears His Owl Glasses

He wears his owl glasses, holds out the paper
spread to the sports or business, frowns
with the effort of concentration against
a tide of feeling. He doesn't know whether

he can resolve this one. All he wants is peace.
The peace of rabbits scrabbling in the wood,
dove pigeons in the morning cool,
the sheep in knee-high grass

waiting for the feed to arrive of a morning,
crying if it is cold, with maybe two hens
clacking about, a jackdaw scooting the hen-
house, and his true love always smiling.

The Boiling Bit

William here runs joyfully to
the camera, where the tobacco
rests and burns, smoulders and releases
its fragrant smoke. He says he hopes he
has not stepped upon my feet. Any
Tom, Dick or Harry can do it. I've
had a visitor. The man from Wook.
He came and said have you seen my cock.
I could not speak because he scared me.
They tell you at the surgery it's
just a prick, it won't hurt, and you look
the other way, and it does. He
was quite the handsomest of men. He
had bought all the wood, but when he got
to that tree, because it was in an
awkward corner, he said I think that
we will just leave the boiling bit. It's
the tough lump off a beast. The butcher
calls them the boiling bits. They only
had axes in those days. I said no,
I have not seen your cock. Describe it.
So he did. I said does he have hens.
He said yes, five, but he fancies yours.
Then I counted ten again. I said
I'd rather you didn't go near ours.
Will's Thing is the electric cable
wound round a metal hand. And as if

it were planned (de-dah, de-dah), the pipe
has a flat hole at one end to go
into the mouth. What a lot of hoo-
hah over a little thing like that.
It's a fallacy cuddling a cat.

June

Evening. A cool June. Hand in hand
we walk round the garden, dodging
loose stones, gaps where the new lawn needs
chocking with ballast, ducking the
windsock wrapping itself round its
pole, checking rows of this and that,
which seeds have failed to show up, which
flowers begin to glow, cold-frame
cucumbers to grow big enough
to finger the panes of glass. But
there is no blossom this year on
the apple tree. It has been too
cold. But when we step round the house
to the front door again and kiss,
we know it is no ordinary
love, this, that we stand in the cold
and the damp of this unusual
cold, wet June (but there are no wars)
and do what we do all the time —
love indoors outdoors just the same.

Viagra

Erecting heavy agricultural machinery
needs care: you wouldn't trifle with a Harley-Davidson,
would you? Veer grasswards on your gleaming, heavier-grade machine,
the weight will throw you flat as a "Live 'ere? Grrrand!" in a devia-gram,
albeit in gorgeous surroundings (vie aggravatingly for them!).

However, when Alston Guardians were told that an order sent
to the workhouse had six quarts of gin included, and Mr. Dowson
said he'd never heard of such a thing, the workhouse master
told him the gin was ordered on the instructions of the doctor.
Happiness will grunt and groan, whatever the gain.

Tommy

"They'll not come here for nine sheep —
it's not worth setting the gear up."
So we got Tommy, and met
him at the town cross at eight-
thirty in the morning. We had
already fetched in the sheep and lambs
from the wood where they hid
themselves. We'd gone down to Billy's
Field, looking for them. The silly
things would have wandered through the gate
and the wind would have blown it shut,
we thought. But no, no sheep or lambs
in Billy's Field. Then we saw them
miles off, down the avenues.
They started running as soon as
they saw us and Fly, who hurtled
her burly body through thistles
and nettles, settling down from time
to time to take orders from
her master following behind.
I walked through the wood to the end
to stop them coming back. They were
scuttling away all together
in a flock towards the gate
opening across to the shed,
where we locked them in and set off,
closing the gate behind us, for

Tommy. Tommy is not dapper
but is a great sheep clipper,
Douglas says. Here he is, his
great hands, feeling the fleece
(he has been grinding the oiled shears
in the shed while we lashed two ewes
to the gate), clipping from the neck
round the belly edge, then back
from the tail end, trim the shitty
bits off. Meanwhile, the skitty
blackface ewe waits placidly
like a duchess sunk on petti-
coats. Tommy meanwhile clips a bit,
stops a bit, pulls half a cig out
and lets the ewe breathe between
rows of tufts of wool and sodden
bits trodden and peed upon
by the ewe who seems quite happy
to be held and sheared by Tommy.

July

"Well, it's certainly raining today."
Walking to the shed on this July
morning under the dunked rain clouds
pelting, pattering, steaming, glowing
and white, on the hills standing head and shoulders
over us, shoulder to shoulder
in the vast cathedral of which this
wood we huddle through in the drizzle
is a simple side chapel,
or even just a pew, or a hole
in the floorboards, from which vantage point
we can see our little things,
hens sheltered in the straw, one
half-size egg in the tabernacle
awaiting us, sheep, half of them
shorn, potatoes, rhubarb shorn by the lambs
of the gods, of the hills, we prepare
ourselves for a sacrament of strawberries,
not quite ripe, but dunked in red-stained sugar
like blood, thicker than
the flood which is Saint Swithun's.

Cherries

Finishing under the cherry tree,
we picked two cherries each and shared
another one. We finished our evening
walk under the cherry tree bobbing
with bright fruit hung like fairy lights, some
of them red. These we reached and tugged from
off their stalks. Each one was bitter, sour,
yet we licked the skin and dragged it off
the flesh, the stone, and chewed the sweetness
there as best we could. We'd gone out
into the cool air, faced the wind
and ended up by the cherry tree.
To our delight we saw that, unlike
anything else in the garden, it was
bearing fruit. They were yellow and shiny,
a few were red, some with brown patches.
We picked them straight off the tree, needing
to tug at the stalks, and then handed
them to each other and rolled our
tongues round the flesh and the slippery
stones within, swallowing it, bitter,
sweet, sour and all. We came back into
the warm house, leaned on the radiator
in the hall and laid our cold cheeks
together, still chewing the bitter
flesh of the cherries, sucking their

shiny skins until there was no more
left in our mouths (we spat the stones out
before chewing) smarting with fresh
saliva, to chew or try to chew,
whichever was possible to do there.

My Lover Gave Me Green Leaves

My lover gave me green leaves
with the mud of the garden on them,
radishes sharp and red,
nasturtium flames.

He gave me the tender heart
of a cabbage, its glossy coat,
a loaf of bread studded deep
with seeds.

He gave me the note
the blackbird
I'd cried at the blackness of
by the river sang.

He gave me the struck fire
of the thoughts
in his mind —
flint on flint.

He gave me the taste,
direct on his tongue,
of the syllables their embers
did not destroy.

He gave me his word,
the word of an Adam —
a promise,
should he set eyes on the sun.

He gave me a drop of the dew
to hold.
To see my face in it.
To look through.

He gave me,
in the chrisomed palm
of his empty hand —
a gasp of joy.

There's Something Going On Here

The phone burred. Douglas went out, returned and laughed.
"It's Richard. He's ten minutes away."

He had eyes like blue dinner plates.
I'd seen them in pictures.
But from where I sat
squinting from one to the other,
from Granddad's flushed face
to where his eyes' beam
dazzled his grandson, he just was
real, hair dark and curly, skin
like a good onion. He'd bought
a house in Leicester and had a new
bird called Karen, who had yet
to meet his mother, who they knew
would give her the once-over.
He went for a walk by the river
and brought back field mushrooms, which he
found on the Flatt Field by the trees,
he said. We ate them next
morning with bacon for breakfast —
though later when we looked for ourselves
in the Flatt Field we found none —
they were delicious. The clothes-
line he saw when he first came down
("Hallo. I'm Jo. And I'm here."
I had said when I opened the door),
and what was on it, and he said,
"There's something going on here, Granddad."

August

The first fine morning of the summer.
I throw wide the kitchen door
to usher a gasp of blown air in
(we've kept the stove alight — nothing is sure)
and step into the space outside, the light, the whisht,
the blue.
After breakfast, the shed. Let out the hens.
Collect two eggs. Cover their food against crows.
Then on down the Flatt Field seeking mushrooms
on the edge of the wood. Two pigeons there.
One, nearly dead, accepts in peace the offered coup.
The other has gone before. "The weather." Douglas says.
A circle of white field mushrooms stands nearby.
We glean the four that glow, gray-gilled,
leave black side up in the muck the maggoty ones,
cross the narrow track the sheep, stepping from Billy's
Field, have beaten into the edge of the Flatt Field,
the bulge of the hanky bundle loosely tied
— later emptied, flak, pine needles and all,
onto the kitchen table. Back to the shed for Jack,
who sits with an unreproachful attention
behind the gate, eager to seek a rabbit
carcass under the willow if allowed
to do so despite his owner's frown.

How Can I Explain to You That He Was Real?

In a lump which banged as it humped,
the last of the lamb came out of the freezer,
deliquesced in the summer heat
in a bowl overnight. Next morning
it slid from its bag, unwrapped
from its thick aroma. With thumbs I prised
the red pool, wet and sweet, ripped
white sinews off a strip of breast meat,
ran the kidneys out of their marble sheath,
found a scrap of liver, drizzled the earth
and shit off the feet with a jet of icy water.
He said:
"Now for the opening up of the heart,
the hollow chamber. You have to open the heart.
Tear the calms from the crucible stains
in the middle, trim off the fat.
Slice it through and open it out
through the wall, the medallions,
blazons of light, the doors which open
on one side only. Reveal the left
and right apartments, the best of rooms,
the choice, the best of the house,
wherein to feed, to lodge, to love."

Two Treasures

I

Because language is difficult for me
I have holes. Read the meaning in my whole.
Look at me. Look through me. I am split,
light gray, bleaching from the tip.
My fate is to stay too long. I turn and change,
turn many ways. I slowly lay down
on the ground till I was found.
The holes are all that is absent.
I want to enclose again, to wrap around
the living flesh of the thistle stem.
But it is gone. One day I will be gone.
You noticed me, saw my meaning
on a particular day. I had been here
a long time. Look at me. Look through me.
I can show you the world. I am a petrified saint.
I am an insect with many eyes.
My holes are my bereavements.
Each one is a grief that I will not forget.
I am a hand held out. I let rain trickle through
like tears. I am a sieve. I encircle light.
I am the angle at which I lie.
If I were an animal, where would be my eye?
If I were the world, where would be my whole?
Walk in under my canopy.
See the light through my windows, feel the rain.

2

It is a lamb's horn off a breed of sheep
no longer living here. So soft and light
when found, it could have been a bleached
stem off a thistle or dock blown deep
into the wood at the height of summer.

You could sink it in a bucket of water for a day
and pin it to the shaft of an ash with a nail.
It would make a sort of shepherd's crook, but what you would do
with it next is more difficult to say —
tickle some creature's tummy, perhaps, that lay asleep.

It could be a pointing finger, or a gasping fish
whose mouth never shuts, as if the pink
interior contained too much for its hidden
spiral to hold and it all spews out
in a black rush as its streaks and lips contort.

It is peeling away from the point in strips.
It is an outer covering, has nothing to give.
It is hollow, the half bone, half horn, inner core stuff gone,
and most of the pink blush worn off the ribs,
and the crown where it tore from the skull paper thin and white.

Annunciation

The sky clears.
The sun melts the ice.
You are cruel.
But I hold you close.

The sun changes.
Your eyes are blue.
You are cruel.
But your words are true.

(What would I change?
You're something else —
beyond goodbye
or true or false.)

I'm wishing blessings down upon
three ewes to go for sale as mutton,
one of them Susan
or Annunciation.

I ask you, can you hear her voice?
You say she's wanting out on the grass.
Well of course!
That's it.

You stand at table writing THREE
GELD CHEVIOT EWES FOR SALE
D. D. I ponder writing J. and D.,
but thereby hangs another tale.

Farewell to Samantha

Up the Horse Pasture I walked,
through the buttercups and cuckoo spit.
I found her grazing alone.
I stroked her silken belly,
ran my fingers over her hard
flat nose, her velvety mouth,
scraped a nail through the cross
in the straggle of her back,
looked into her fathomless
wet peat eyes.
I sat under her chin
and let her chew my hair.
I ran my fingers up and down
her forelegs till clumps of down
drifted away. She paused,
then continued to pull
and surround with her mouth
the tufts of grass. I rose
and walked back. She followed,
keeping to her own worn furrow.
I turned her out at the gate
and enclosed her in the pen,
then gave her a bowl of barley and maize,
and a bucket of water.

Banks of Clouds

Banks of clouds hover just above the pale
horizon, under the burning sun.
Everywhere, long shadows. I walk down
to Bleagate. Two Land Rovers. Not a soul.
Then the gate to Varty's Field, with Jack. No
sign of the dreaded cattle. We pass through.
Tractor tracks carve up the field. My feet are lost
in their tread punched deep in the mud and grass.
Curving lines of black plastic shrink-wrapped
hay bales, then a thin sheep track and churned
clarts where cattle have recently been kept
fidgeting at the gate. Wood betony,
Self-heal flower by the Tyne. Which roars. I had
intended a paddle but thought better
when I saw the brown turmoil, the stewed
froth of heather tea coiling its muscular
bulk at the bottom of the valley.
Ominous with their heavy cargo of shadows,
the clouds hang over Cross Fell, its hard line inky
black, rolled out like a pair of bony shoulders
carved in stone on a tomb. This coming visit
casts a shadow of the past before it —
events so painful there can be no response,
no knowledge where to go thence.

September

Tootsies cold in boots. September.
Cold lamb and salad and bread and butter.

Drink at the Turks Head. Celebrate.
Walk upriver to Gossipgate.
Susan's got a baby, Amelia.
Happy Families. Twenty Questions. Peter,

washing up last thing at night,
questions. Must not rise to the bait.
Shed the sheep, put lambs in the field.
Whisky at midnight. Concentrate.

Hug the kids goodbye at the shed.
Come back and find pink sheets on the bed.
All's well. Green Door with sixty more.
Cow with a sad bull yells like a chainsaw.

Has your sister been and gone?
Changing of bed linen — pink sheets on.
January, February, March, April, May.
Future and past no longer matter.

Sheila and Jack

I jumped up naked, then remembered:
Douglas had said "Wait here."

The couple stand in the window
looking at Scarberry Hill. I run
back to the bedroom, don some clothes
before they can see me. They've been expected
this past six months, and now they come
this afternoon and find us in bed!
They knock at the door. It's answered
by their cousin in bath towel, using
the first excuse that comes to his head,
i.e., "We're in the bath, just a mo,
we'll get some clothes on, do come in."
Meanwhile, I'd assumed all clear, but no.
I straighten shirt, go in, kiss both.
A moment of awkwardness, then sweet-
ness and light. We all forget the 'bath.'
(It barely, if at all, improves the truth.)
Crisp polka dots is like her cousin's mum
I think. Her better half slumps in red,
still gobsmacked. I put on all my charm.
Chat re her cousin as a lad,
the girls when small, hols on the farm.
Swimming at Barnard Castle (not bad,
twice a week, for eighty-one or so).
The brothers lost in the war. "Sad times"
she says. Then raspberries: they grow

them by the bucket. Would have brought more
had they only known their cousin
is no longer alone. They gulp and stare
as the full implications of
the afternoon's events sink in —
as they assess me for the walk-on part I'll have.

There's a Stream Outside the Gate

There's a stream outside the gate.
Here is a bucket. Go and fetch some water.
Too much. Tip half out.
You will now prepare the smut-nosed ewe for slaughter.

Then wash this hogg's guts
and smear them with oil and strap them tight.
I'll leave you to it
but I'll still cut her throat.

You will bury her yourself.
You're not finished though.
Cut this ash with a jackknife,
it'll make a good stick.

Rip up these nettles
or I'll do something sick.
Take a spade and the lamb
and bury her — quick.

You will hold a ewe still
without touching her head.
You will keep the fridge full
without leaving our bed.

Goats have no trouble
in wet wind and raw.
We'll feed her on rubble,
she'll bed without straw.

She 'll make all our milk
or her throat will be cut.
You'll keep yourself in
and you'll keep your cats out.

And if you do?
I will love you.
If you eat of this bread
that I give to you.

There Was a Darkness in the Air

There was a darkness in the air,
I looked and saw it speak,
felt it waiting by my back,
not savagery . . . but near.

It was like an autumn slack
sharpening the air.
Its shadow shone beneath the black
as if the sun were there.

It muscled in, as meek
a line, as black and sleek
as lack of light, a smothered laugh,
a sudden lifted care.

It was ramrod straight
from standing still in fear.
The pain that chilled the hallway
had suffocated dare.

It was the father who was gone,
the wife who went before,
the brother who is never seen,
the sister at the door.

The Lambs Were Still Running with the Ewes

The lambs were still running with the ewes when we killed
the fattest male. Three lambs and one ewe had been penned
in since the day before (you don't pen one alone
or they fret). "Turn him round!" Then, quickly, as I held
his head and collar, Jackson stuck the butcher's knife
into his neck, whereupon torrents of dark red
fluid gushed bubbling, frothing into a bucket.
It looked not so much like blood as mulberry juice.
We'd wondered whether to wait for the rain to fine,
then thought, what the hell, and went out straightaway in
the blowing rain, which was sculpting itself in the
pine needles. We'd stuffed wool into the eaves of the
loose box to keep out the rain only that morning.
(The oils from the wool stuck to our fingers. The dust
I blew off the books was precious. Once upon a
time they would be sheep vellum. Now they had narrow
rims of sheep oil instead at the top of the page.)
Jackson had decided on one of two brothers.
(The third was the lamb of the ewe, less fat.) This lamb
did not struggle (couldn't) or utter a sound. He
was the fatter of the two brothers. We released
the ewe and the two lambs, who went straight to the grass.
Jackson got into the race with the chosen lamb,
fastened a collar on his neck, then a rope, and
I opened the gate. Out he came, bucking, pulling.
I got behind and pushed him on his way. Jackson
went on to the loose box, where the bench and the knives

had been made ready. I grabbed him by the back feet.
This was wrong. I was to grab his fleece. Then Jackson
got him on his back and bound his front feet, then one
hind foot to them. As the blood drained out and the eyes
clouded over and closed, the thrashing of his hooves
continued. I dodged them and held on to him tight.
Then there came the moment when, with many violent
rasps, he breathed his last. He was desperate to breathe.
Then Jackson started to skin him. First one foreleg
he slit and broke off at the joint, then the other,
then slit to the middle, down with a zipping sound,
and the lower legs the same, eased the skin off round
his tummy, then hauled him up (didn't want him on
the floor if possible), with a notched bar and rope,
to a metal beam. We heaved and pulled, for he was
very bulky and heavy, and his head, with its
enormous mulberry hole, still dragged on the ground.
Jackson set to work with his skinning knife, slashing
bit by bit, working the skin off, pulling between
times, exposing the glistening pearly fat and
often the rosy pink flesh too. I tugged the skin
at the neck, then, with a saw and a knife, we cut
the head off. We hauled him onto the bench. Jackson
cut off the balls first, left the liver and lights to
deal with later, rolled the fleece and stuffed it into
a feedbag, cut and tied esophagus and wind-
pipe, then slit him right down the middle and let all

the opal-green innards slide out and stomach bag
burst its green flood on the floor. Clean and separate.
Beads of black shit. White lace caul. I held back the two
thin curtains of his stomach while Jackson foraged
round inside with hand and knife. We dragged him next door,
still very heavy, but now without the bulge of
stomach. Coming back, we were about to go through
the gate when Jackson said "Spuds!" Went back for a fork,
squelched around in wellies in the spud bed to find
a likely forkful. I picked them, knuckle white, from
the clarts, and put them in a bread bag. On the way
home Jackson emptied them into a torrent of
rain by the roadside and let them tumble clean in
the water, helped on by his boots and my fingers.

October

Six fresh ewes stood in the shed, bewildered.
We opened the gate. They trundled through,
ran crazily here and there on the Flatt Field.
The dog brought the others up from Billy's Field to join them.

Let's move, go, hie, gang, roll,
                    drift, chug, explore.
I'm faint. You're a hinny. I'm not.
                    Mm . . . buttery. Test the sap for edibility.
This faintness . . . I'm groggy, hipshot.
                    Hallo! Flesh eater or herbivore?

Grind the cud. Dung: avoid.
                    Hey! a salt lick.
Must git some belly timber,
                    gobbets in ma moof.
Dabbled in the marsh. Mere pap.
                    A salt lick!
Grab the grass. Sip, sip.

Time to git a nib, a quid, sugar
                    her with the lump of coal on her nose.
Flat Pap dips her mush in the water.
                    There's asphalt there.

Freaks!
                    Jag, tug, wrench.

With nippers, winkle out,
                mumble, champ and peck.
It'll do. Just tucker.

This ewe lamb
             is in the clouds,
giddy with thinking
               of wool in the spring.
A wobbler, a blink, a dimp.

A flock of sheep like a flotilla of clouds
in the sky silently tend their grass crop in an autumn
haze. They tear at it, squeeze it, suck down
the sugary juice (not much right now), tamp
it down with pronged hooves, then fertilize
it with shit. Then wander on to the next bit.

At the Elk's Head

My stomach ached for the hole, the bloody
lump in your head. I set you down.
You took off your cap. The landlady
ran to us, eager to help. We sat
with knees and elbows together in the window,
holding on to your life. In the window
a *Vanessa atalanta* cowered
in the corner of a pane on the beveled
inner edge as if to get as far from the
space in the center of the room as
possible. I picked it up and cupped my palm
around it, elbowed my way out
through the door to the garden,
to a privet facing our window, tried
to shake it out, but the butterfly clung.
Its two little suckers, prong by prong,
held on. By the corner of a wing
in the tips of finger and thumb
I plucked it off my palm
and set it down in the leaves.
In a flutter it was gone.

November

He trots in every morning
with the fluorescent mark
on his back. The first couple
of times, it was tentative,
after he'd fed with the ewes,
but now he appears by the
gate at the start of feeding
time. He gets plenty of maize
as well as black nuts, which
is what he likes. The hens go
bananas. There's always more
than enough both for him and
for them. He is so tiny
he doesn't look as if he'll
ever fatten up. He stands
apart always from the ewes,
even from his twin sister.
He cannot understand where
the three other wethers have
gone (they went to market in
Carlisle last week). He comes in
every morning full of hope
for his morning feed. One day
he will come in and be killed.
Will he know when that's to be?
Marra, do you know when you
too will die, or even how?

Heart

The first time I killed a lamb, his heart kept
beating after we'd cut his throat and opened
up his chest. It rose and fell with a leap
that slowly diminished till it was like the lift
and fall of a leaf. I'd expected a sort of hard
red stone set in marble there in the middle, and so
I thought him alive still. You said, "No, dear heart,
it's a reflex." And when we returned, it was gone. His heart
beat barely a season and a half, and so
was reluctant to stop. So when you spilled your seed
on my heart from above and below, my heart remembered,
and began its final lap of beating.

Your Way

I

How long does it take to reach the end of the lane,
almost stationary, frozen? You tell me, "Go
ahead and feed the ewes." I get my jar and catch
you up, take longer than I thought. But you are there
still, moving barely perceptibly, just slightly
swaying side to side. By the time you reach the shed
the sheep are fed. You had said, "Walk on. I shall be
very slow. I shall take a long time." As distant
galaxies cross our horizon, their image will
be frozen. And when you tell me to "bugger off,
go do the job," under your rough gob is concern.
You often say "Go on," but often I say "No."
For I like to walk with you, your way, more slowly
than the elephant, as a galaxy at the
end of time, faster than the speed of light, so you
are swinging out of ken faster than glances can
any more pass between, faster than I can see
any longer, than I can ever catch you up.

2

How long does it take to reach the end of the lane?
You are near the end as we watch the galaxies
fade, their appearance frozen in time. I tell you,
"Go ahead, I'll see that the fire's OK," as they
recede from us. But you are there still, are frozen,
moving barely perceptibly under the trees,
your dark form gathered in the shade. As we watch the
galaxies fade, just slightly swaying side to side,
by the time you reach the shed the sheep are fed, their
appearance frozen in time. If I can ever
catch you up to taste your lips, put my arms round you,
distant galaxies will then be moving too fast.
You say "Go on." As distant galaxies
cross our horizon will I ever catch up with
you? The end of the universe, frozen in time
as we watch, will never be able to reach us.

3

You tell me, "Go ahead, for they will never grow
older or change. They will only grow dimmer as
they recede from us." Then when I come up to the
lane I expect to find it bare, but you are there,
your dark form gathered, too fast for me to see. As
distant galaxies cross our horizon, the light
they emit after the moment of horizon
crossing will never be able to reach us. As
we watch the galaxies fade, which you so often
forget, you say, "Walk on. I shall be very slow.
I shall take a long time." You often say "You go
on," but often I say "No." For I like to walk
slowly, your way, this majestic way you exist
and travel through this space on the lane by the trees.

4

How long does it take to reach the end of the lane?
As we watch the galaxies on the way back, the
glob of blood glistens on the tarmac where you coughed,
and although animals later lick up the blood
the dark patch stays next morning when the tarmac is
frozen. And when you tell me to "bugger off, go
do the job," under your rough gob is concern. I
love the way you move so slowly that your mind sees
things differently. You often say "You go on,"
but often I say "No." I like to walk slowly
with you, your way, more slowly than the elephant,
as a galaxy at the frozen end of time.

December (*Christmas Box*)

We go feed the lambs. The wether
we were fattening for slaughter
is not there. I go look for him.
He lies apart. I stroke his head.
He stumbles to his feet. I drive
him to where the other lambs stand
and eat. He won't look at the food,
stood with his back to them. He has
a look of profound disgust in
his eyes. We bathe the ewe's feet. I
splash my eye. It stings. Snow swims in
shoals. We bury the lamb, go home.
We baptize him with a trickle
of water I coaxed from the stream
in a bucket. Stretched out and cold.
On the Horse Pasture, eyes open.
In the top far corner, on a
marshy piece of ground. Between the
stream and a marshy piece of ground.
With a crock of gold at each ear.
A rainbow hat to make a crock
of gold at each ear. A magic
dress for shepherding in the snow.
Gloves, striped green and blue. A velvet
and gold satin scarf. A magic
box of swords, a survival tool.
He lies apart. I stroke his head.

Two Feet in a Sack

When you walk down the lane on a crisp winter's
morning following thick snowfall, hand in hand,
footprints behind, virgin snow around, and you
want to see your footprints and you look behind,
you have to stop, the footprints stop. What you find
is that you must twist around and your footprints
are smeared in the snow, lose the shape of your feet,
and you cannot move because your partner is
just standing there, is gazing at you fondly
wondering what you are doing, or, like you,
is looking back. It's like two feet in a sack.
If one turns, the other can't stay back. We walked
down the lane holding hands. You held my hand tight
and swept on ahead, but I kept looking back.

I Thought You'd Gone to the River

"It was a great shock to me, pet, when I discovered
that you were off, gone to the river. Where's
all the water? Weren't you down at Gossipgate?"

After the reading, I left Gossipgate and came home.
He stood smiling in the backlit doorway, in the frost
of December. And yet, I never did find out which
of the farms whose names were rough-printed in my notebook —
Hartsop Hall, Grove Farm, Beckstones, Crook-a-Beck, Deedale Hall,
Greenbank, Noran Bank, Side Farm, Braestead, Gillside, Home Farm,
Glencoyne — and which he had worked for six months at a time
as a hired lad of sixteen in the '20s, would bring a smile
of recognition to his face, the boy in the photo at Gossipgate,
perched, legs spread, on the fourth and fifth Sisters, water
spurting between his legs, a fag dangled
out of the right corner of his mouth, a flower
in his buttonhole, jacket flared on the stones, a giant
flat cap like a pudding on his head, next to two other youths
with no cigarettes whose booted feet crossed right
to left, and all with equally delicate and beautiful
hands, so the grandson of this one on his far right uses
them now to mix alloys in melting pots, but for his
he was much sought after amongst the farmers and their wives
to go inside the ewes and pull out their lambs,
and the water gushes out between his legs
even now, though once he did take me to Patterdale,
and we sat in the White Lion where he said they would congregate
seventy years ago and there'd be plates of ham and beef

laid out on the black polished table, the lads would help
themselves, unpeel on their forks the slivers of grainy
flesh in this room where we were sitting behind
the shutters after looking at the angled light on the lake
near stone basins lined with moss and holding green
cloudy water, the blue slate stones, and beech and ash,
abundant ferns, and bridges, the thin line of water
between the tree roots in the narrow aperture of the valley,
the crosshatched stones, green fillets, streaks, blue shadows,
red and white stripes, meadowsweet and birch, bracken,
wood sorrel in the tiny cracks, angled rock
thickly lichen-skinned, where Herdwick scrambled
on the stony soil, and the thought of shepherding
on those vertiginous fields made me feel queasy sick,
and the rain-spotted stones, the mountain knuckles above
the trees, the pathway up through the ferns, the sheep
bone bundle, browned with a gray tail, beetle scratchings,
two sailboats slowly parting on the water between
the trees, near the islands, rows of silver birch
drooping, leaves cascading, larch and beech
dipping slowly, and under the chestnut glossy leaves.

January

Midnight. A stranger at the door,
clutching a coal and coin.
He knocks a bit before we hear.
What say we let him in?

Yes, he has bitter oranges,
sugar, lemons too.
Yes, he could crib a jackdaw's song,
crack it against a tooth.

Yes, he could snap it in his grip,
yes, he would cuss at first.
Blood be bitten, spat and wiped,
his patient ordered rest.

But there will be no rest today
(midnight has paid its debt).
He shall eat grass and sup the clay
("Tastes good but's full of grit").

Breathing

As I walk up the rise into the silence of snow, in the sough of brittle
    snowflakes,
you are breathing shallow breaths in bed.
A paper tissue lies discarded where I dabbed a drip from your nose.

As I sit in another room you are swishing your lips.
You have become the inside of my body. I am gasping for the crackle
and whistle of your chest. My body is your world under a blanket
    of snow.

The wolf leaves paw prints on it, catching a niff of tussocky breasts,
dipping thighs, flat tummy, tight skin, the mutter of a bony outcrop.
Hills rise and fall with your breathing, its spate and its whisper.

The snow is lisping from the eaves as I listen for the blab of your heart.
You stir to speak. Your chest heaves. Fistfuls of ice slack off and pelt
    the stones,
sluds of snow stretch and slide under the window.

There is a quiver, a tingle, then icy water stutters after the snow in
    a stream.
The night before last, you stopped.
There was a gulp, then stillness and listening — for the lick

of the meniscus on a swollen river, for a trickle in the dried-out bed
of a beck, the jostle of fingertips, snapping of feet. You nestled
    in a heap
under jacket, quilt, hat, light, scarf, shawl, sheet,

you were all twined and tangled up,
your suck held back by a puff, a spanking sea breeze,
then, flat out, pillows concertinaed, released a salty waft, a redolence

while you held one slippered foot under the sinews, stung and docketed
the twisted jumble, face motionless apart from spitting pith,
and I hoicked you up, straightened the pillows in your shadow

and your voice spurted out as I kibbled your lungs in my own chest's
    thump.
A sky flipped open when you breathed again, like the tilt over Hartside
    Top.
No birds. No scratchings. Just rustling of clothes and clacking of teeth.

February

Why did you make a heart like me?
Big, red, floppy, ugly,
not even heart-shaped, particularly.
If you prop me on the picture rail I'll flop.
If I'm pinned above the TV I'll be binned
within a day or two, you'll see.

Tomorrow is Saint Valentine's Day.
I have made my valentine —
a huge but imperfect heart
wrapped in string,
labeled TO and FROM.
A big red heart
in brown paper and red crêpe.

How did you make a heart like me?
Big, red, floppy, ugly,
not even heart shaped, particularly.
If you prop me on the picture rail I'll flop.
If I'm pinned above the TV I'll be binned
within a day or two, you'll see.

I smoothed the brown paper
on the kitchen table, folded it in two,
drew a half heart shape,
cut it out and opened it,
then with another,

slightly bigger, in red crêpe,
hapt the brown heart,
folded down the edges
and stuck it with glue.
Rather messy,
but it does look like a heart.
I wrote a message
in pencil on the back,
then rolled up the lot
and tied it with string.

What will you do with a heart like me?
Big, red, floppy, ugly,
not even heart-shaped, particularly.
If you prop me on the picture rail I'll flop.
If I'm pinned above the TV I'll be binned
within a day or two, you'll see.

We Three

In the patients' parlor Les struggles up for a pee.
Douglas at once starts the torturous process of setting
weight on his feet, pressing white-knuckled
on the arms of his chair, tautening strings in his knees,

and I, on my feet already, hang on to Douglas
by his quaking elbows as he extends a hand
to Les. For a long moment we three stand,
there we are, we three,

a row of scarecrows, a flapping line
of clothes, till Les, finally steady,
solo exits the door to left, but a moment later,
a chiding nurse on his arm, reappears.

The Last Time You Came Home

You were sitting in the patients' parlor.
Bob met me outside in the sunshine,
very excited. "He's been promoted."
I looked at the bed. It was stripped
down to blue. So it was true.
You were coming home.
A young nurse helped.
We put you in the front.
Did you want the soft tartan
fleece wrapped right round?
No, you said. I locked the door
your side, drove really slowly
in the spring sunshine, especially
past Beverley's ponies. You did
look at them. But when I turned
at the shed and said the sheep are there,
you did not respond. I parked
so you were next to the gate,
levered you out, feet,
hands, head, lean on the gate,
shuffle on the path, a rush
of slow steps, grasp the knobbly
rail, sway, hold you,
clutch you round the waist,
over the doorstep. Stop.
Pause to drop hat, coat,
take stick further, to the light

round the corner, to the fire,
reach chair, seize the arm, twist
slowly round, sink, back,
into softness. Is it good
to be home? It's great, you said.

Nothing More

After they took you back to hospital
I wept in the empty house by the billowing bed.
Later, I walked with Jack up the hill to see the edge
of the flat stream crinkle with ice.
Then came to see you. "Father . . . ," you said, "next door . . .
Needn't say anything. Survey the mines.
Put this pony on for me. I want to pack
it in. I'm too old now at sixty-four."
Next day you smiled and winked and said, "I love
you. How are your winnings on the horses? They won't
let me out. I want to be out." Next day, on my way
to the reading, you said, "You go on . . . be back quick. You look
perfect." After the reading you said, "I was thinking
of you the whole time." The next day you said, "Get the ladder
so I can climb out. Clear the way up there. I've not
been here all night. I've been walking about, working.
Write and ask her where I am. The window
might go up and down. I just want to get
through it if I can. Is there some Christmas
whisky? The cows are going in a string — see
them walking. I want a hat — and a tie. Just a short
ladder and I could be out. Push that window
right open and see what happens. Take your pullover off.
She says her mother cannot get out. We're stuck
here. I cannot get out of the bed. You've got a husband
locked up in the bloody mine . . . Tell them to get
their bloody selves in . . . here Jo . . . this one . . . I'm tired . . .

Douglas is sailing through the time. I thought
you said there was none, but next year, or when it's time,
I'll bag some coals, or bag some whisky. Your little
hand, was it? Hands in winter. Get up and have
a look. They're floating in and out of water.
There's a little door there. Jo! . . . Jo! . . . Wait
a minute. I'm fine. I love you." Many kisses.
You take a glass of grapefruit juice in your violently
shuddering hand, in the end turn it upside down
on the bed, say, "It got spilt." Then "I had a bath
yesterday and a shave and everything. I won't
have a bath tonight." When I said that I was going
home soon and was that all right and would
you be good and eat your breakfast, you nodded sweetly.
Your eyes shone as though by their own gray light, your body
danced in their flicker, you spread your arm out more
than once in an amazed showing, absorbed by what
you were seeing. You seemed to be at once in a sort
of trance yet fully aware of what was around you.
I read you a couple of Sommer poems: "Worldliness"
(got a smile and a nod), "Potatoes" (spuds . . . your line . . .
you nodded, but stopped me halfway through). You tried
to get out of bed, you lifted your feet from the sheets
and said, "I'm happy with my own thoughts, pet. You go
and feed the hens, I'll follow on." At lunch
you'd eaten some morsels of baked potato, a sliver
of tomato, spitting out the skin in my hand.

At teatime you swallowed three or four small spoonsful
of carrot soup. But when I offered you bread
and tea and custard, you said, "Nothing more . . .
Nothing." So when the phone rang that night not long after
I got home, I knew what it was. As I laid
my head on your still warm tummy, on your still warm tummy
was the shiny, crinkly plaster holding the line
and the needle still full of saline, inscribed *18.00 15.3.04.*

There Were Rainbows Every Day

There were rainbows every day
for three or four days afterward.
I sat in the large soft bed
with silence and stillness falling
around me like snow. Cross Fell
was icy white with a shock
of frozen cloud on its uppermost
tip. The carpet by the bed,
washed several times on the last
day you were home, took a week
to dry to a nubbly paperiness.
The henhouse filled with wind,
the roof was ripped away.
First one side of it split
open, then the other.
The garden shed blew apart,
the timbers of the frame rattled loose.
Rain lashed the windows.
The trees strained. The back door
blew open. Greenhouse glass
smashed. You were beautiful.
Your forehead smelled of powdered
millstone grits and moss.
Your ruby lips and throat
glistened. A red dot stood
on your eyebrow. (Did I nick
you slightly when I snipped

those troublesome hairs you'd swiped
me off from trimming?) Your Top
Man shirt and navy soft wool
waistcoat. A barely visible
smudge on your chin where the last
few mouthfuls of soup spooned in
had dribbled out again.
Your gray eyes dry and sinking,
like a Grünewald's overcome with wonder.

Where Were You When I Came In from the Evening Milking?

Where were you when I came in from the evening milking?
Your chair sat empty by the fire, its cushion hollow,
And each room in the house was empty also.
Where were you?

You were not in any of the house's rooms.
I looked carefully in each one.
And the window view each looked out upon was empty.
Where were you?

The mossy garden path stepped empty round
the corners of the house.
Thyme, ramsons, rosemary leapt in the breeze.
Where were you?

I thought I glimpsed you once in your cap, slowly shuffling on,
face down, intent on the cobbles.
You did not see me — the light shone through and you were gone.
Where were you?

I stood outside the house and looked in where a star shone
from the west straight into the mirror.
I thought for a second you were standing there.
It was not you, it was the setting sun.

Author's Note

I would like to thank Galway Kinnell, Michael Collier and Larry Cooper for their generous and indispensable help with my manuscript. Thanks to both Bobbie Bristol and Galway Kinnell for their friendship, and for making the book possible. I am also grateful for the help and support of the Authors' Foundation (for the award of a grant), the Wordsworth Trust, Margaret and Peter Whyte, Elizabeth Stott, Tom Pickard, M. R. Peacocke, Rebecca O'Connor, Matthew Hollis, Hilary Fell and Stephen Gorton.

•

Grateful acknowledgment is made for permission to reprint the following poems from the author's books published in the United Kingdom:

Scarberry Hill (The Rialto, 2001): "Down Two Fields," "March," "Apple Pie," "Scarberry Hill," "April," "Do I Sleep with You?" "May," "He Wears His Owl Glasses," "The Boiling Bit," "June," "Tommy," "July," "Cherries," "There's Something Going On Here," "August," "A Treasure ('Because language is difficult for me')," "Banks of Clouds," "There's a Stream Outside the Gate," "There Was a Darkness," "The Lambs Were Still Running with the Ewes," "November," "December (Christmas Box)," "Two Feet in a Sack," "January," "February."

The Voice (Flambard Press, 2004): "The Bargain," "A Treasure ('It is a lamb's horn')," "Annunciation," "Farewell to Samantha," "Sheila and Jack," "October," "Your Way," "Where Were You When I Came In from the Evening Milking?"

Several poems previously appeared in the following journals and magazines:

The Independent on Sunday: "Sheila and Jack." *The New Yorker:* "There Were Rainbows Every Day." *Reactions:* "Your Way." *The Rialto:* "April," "He Wears His Owl Glasses," "December (Christmas Box)," "There Was a Darkness in the Air." *Tideline:* "A Treasure ('It is a lamb's horn . . .')."